50 Premium Chinese Noodle Dishes

By: Kelly Johnson

Table of Contents

- Zhajiang Mian (Noodles with Soybean Paste)
- Chongqing Xiaomian (Spicy Noodles)
- Lanzhou Beef Noodles
- Dan Dan Noodles
- Fried Chow Mein
- Sichuan Cold Noodles
- Wonton Noodles
- Beijing Zhajiang Mian (Beijing Noodles)
- Egg Noodles with Peking Duck
- Hand-Pulled Noodles (Lami)
- Guizhou Sour Spicy Noodles
- Cantonese Beef Chow Fun
- Scallion Oil Noodles
- Stewed Pork Belly Noodles
- Beef Brisket Noodles
- Noodles with Shrimp and Scallions
- Cantonese Noodle Soup
- Spicy Sichuan Noodles
- Shrimp Wonton Noodles
- Taiwanese Beef Noodle Soup
- Pork and Chive Dumplings with Noodles
- Dry Fried Noodles with Vegetables
- Hong Kong-Style Noodles with Char Siu
- Red Oil Noodles
- Shanghai Scallion Noodles
- Hot and Sour Noodles
- Luosifen (Snail Rice Noodles)
- Taiwanese Beef Noodles with Pickled Mustard Greens
- Crab Meat Noodles
- Vegetarian Stir-Fried Noodles
- Dan Dan Mian (Chongqing Spicy Noodles)
- Stir-Fried Udon Noodles
- Wonton Soup with Egg Noodles
- Shandong Handmade Noodles
- Yunnan Cross-Bridge Rice Noodles

- Noodles with Sesame Paste
- Beijing Cold Noodles
- Stir-Fried Beef Noodles with Garlic
- Sesame Oil Noodles
- Braised Pork Noodles
- Shrimp Lo Mein
- Steamed Noodles with Oyster Sauce
- Vegetable Noodle Soup
- Chinese Egg Drop Noodle Soup
- Braised Beef Noodles
- Soy Sauce Stir-Fried Noodles
- Fish-Flavored Egg Noodles
- Sichuan Sesame Noodles
- Peking Style Hand-Pulled Noodles
- Hoisin Noodles with Duck

Zhajiang Mian (Noodles with Soybean Paste)

Ingredients:

- 200g Chinese wheat noodles
- 1/2 lb ground pork or beef
- 2 tablespoons fermented soybean paste (or yellow bean paste)
- 1 tablespoon soy sauce
- 1 tablespoon hoisin sauce
- 1 teaspoon sugar
- 2 cloves garlic, minced
- 1/4 cup cucumber, julienned
- 1/4 cup scallions, chopped
- 1 tablespoon sesame oil

Instructions:

1. Cook noodles according to package instructions and set aside.
2. Heat sesame oil in a pan and sauté garlic until fragrant. Add the ground pork or beef and cook until browned.
3. Stir in the soybean paste, soy sauce, hoisin sauce, and sugar. Simmer for 5 minutes until the sauce thickens.
4. Serve the noodles topped with the sauce, cucumber, and scallions.

Chongqing Xiaomian (Spicy Noodles)

Ingredients:

- 200g wheat noodles
- 1 tablespoon vegetable oil
- 2 tablespoons soy sauce
- 1 tablespoon rice vinegar
- 1 teaspoon Sichuan peppercorns
- 1 tablespoon chili oil
- 1/2 teaspoon sugar
- 2 cloves garlic, minced
- 1/4 cup crushed peanuts (optional)
- 2 tablespoons chopped scallions

Instructions:

1. Cook noodles and set aside.
2. Heat oil in a pan and fry garlic until fragrant, add Sichuan peppercorns and chili oil.
3. Add soy sauce, rice vinegar, and sugar, mixing well.
4. Toss noodles in the sauce, top with peanuts and scallions, and serve.

Lanzhou Beef Noodles

Ingredients:

- 200g hand-pulled noodles or egg noodles
- 1/2 lb beef shank or brisket
- 2 cloves garlic, minced
- 1 small onion, sliced
- 2 tablespoons soy sauce
- 2 tablespoons rice wine
- 1 teaspoon five-spice powder
- 4 cups beef broth
- 1/4 cup cilantro, chopped
- 1/4 cup green onions, chopped
- 2 tablespoons chili oil

Instructions:

1. Cook noodles and set aside.
2. In a pot, simmer beef with garlic, onion, soy sauce, rice wine, and five-spice powder for 2 hours until tender.
3. Remove the beef, slice thinly, and set aside.
4. Strain the broth and return to the pot. Bring it back to a simmer.
5. Serve noodles in a bowl, topped with beef slices, broth, cilantro, green onions, and chili oil.

Dan Dan Noodles

Ingredients:

- 200g wheat noodles
- 1/2 lb ground pork
- 2 tablespoons soy sauce
- 1 tablespoon rice vinegar
- 1 tablespoon chili paste or chili oil
- 1 tablespoon sesame paste or peanut butter
- 2 cloves garlic, minced
- 1 teaspoon Sichuan peppercorns, ground
- 1/4 cup scallions, chopped
- 1 tablespoon roasted peanuts, crushed (optional)

Instructions:

1. Cook noodles and set aside.
2. In a pan, cook ground pork with garlic until browned.
3. Add soy sauce, rice vinegar, chili paste, sesame paste, and Sichuan peppercorns. Stir to combine.
4. Toss cooked noodles in the sauce and top with scallions and peanuts.

`

Fried Chow Mein

Ingredients:

- 200g chow mein noodles (fresh or pre-cooked)
- 1/2 lb chicken, beef, or pork, thinly sliced
- 1/4 cup bell peppers, sliced
- 1/4 cup onions, sliced
- 2 cloves garlic, minced
- 2 tablespoons soy sauce
- 1 tablespoon oyster sauce
- 1 tablespoon sesame oil
- 1/4 cup cabbage, shredded
- 1 tablespoon green onions, chopped

Instructions:

1. Cook noodles and set aside.
2. In a pan, heat sesame oil and sauté garlic, then add meat and cook until browned.
3. Add bell peppers, onions, and cabbage. Stir-fry for a few minutes until vegetables are tender.
4. Add soy sauce, oyster sauce, and noodles. Stir to coat the noodles in the sauce.
5. Garnish with green onions and serve.

Sichuan Cold Noodles

Ingredients:

- 200g wheat noodles
- 2 tablespoons soy sauce
- 1 tablespoon rice vinegar
- 1 tablespoon chili oil
- 1 tablespoon sesame oil
- 2 teaspoons sugar
- 1 teaspoon Sichuan peppercorns, ground
- 1/4 cup cucumber, julienned
- 1/4 cup carrots, julienned
- 2 tablespoons chopped scallions

Instructions:

1. Cook noodles and rinse under cold water to cool them.
2. In a bowl, combine soy sauce, rice vinegar, chili oil, sesame oil, sugar, and Sichuan peppercorns.
3. Toss noodles in the dressing, then top with cucumber, carrots, and scallions.
4. Serve chilled.

Wonton Noodles

Ingredients:

- 200g egg noodles
- 12-15 wonton wrappers, filled with shrimp or pork filling
- 1/4 cup soy sauce
- 2 tablespoons sesame oil
- 1 tablespoon rice vinegar
- 1 tablespoon sugar
- 2 cloves garlic, minced
- 1/4 cup bok choy, chopped
- 2 tablespoons green onions, chopped

Instructions:

1. Cook noodles and set aside.
2. In a pot, bring water to a boil and cook wontons for 3-4 minutes until they float.
3. In a separate bowl, combine soy sauce, sesame oil, rice vinegar, sugar, and garlic.
4. Toss cooked noodles with sauce, and top with wontons, bok choy, and green onions.

Beijing Zhajiang Mian (Beijing Noodles)

Ingredients:

- 200g wheat noodles
- 1/2 lb ground pork
- 2 tablespoons soybean paste (or yellow bean paste)
- 1 tablespoon soy sauce
- 1 tablespoon sugar
- 1 tablespoon hoisin sauce
- 1 tablespoon vegetable oil
- 1/4 cup cucumber, julienned
- 1/4 cup scallions, chopped

Instructions:

1. Cook noodles and set aside.
2. Heat oil in a pan and sauté ground pork until browned.
3. Stir in soybean paste, soy sauce, hoisin sauce, and sugar. Simmer for 5 minutes.
4. Serve noodles topped with the sauce, cucumber, and scallions.

Egg Noodles with Peking Duck

Ingredients:

- 200g egg noodles
- 1/2 lb Peking duck, shredded
- 1 tablespoon hoisin sauce
- 1 tablespoon soy sauce
- 2 teaspoons sugar
- 2 cloves garlic, minced
- 1/4 cup cucumbers, thinly sliced
- 1/4 cup green onions, chopped
- 1 tablespoon sesame oil

Instructions:

1. Cook egg noodles according to package instructions and set aside.
2. Shred Peking duck and set aside.
3. In a pan, heat sesame oil and sauté garlic until fragrant.
4. Add hoisin sauce, soy sauce, and sugar, then toss in the duck to heat through.
5. Serve noodles with shredded duck, cucumber, and green onions.

Hand-Pulled Noodles (Lami)

Ingredients:

- 200g all-purpose flour
- 1/2 teaspoon salt
- 1/4 cup water
- 1 tablespoon vegetable oil
- 1 tablespoon sesame oil

Instructions:

1. In a bowl, combine flour and salt. Gradually add water and knead into a dough. Let it rest for 30 minutes.
2. After resting, divide the dough into small balls and roll them out into long ropes. Pull each rope into noodles.
3. Boil a pot of water and cook the noodles for 2-3 minutes until they float to the top. Drain and set aside.
4. Heat sesame oil in a pan, toss in the noodles, and stir-fry for a few minutes before serving.

Guizhou Sour Spicy Noodles

Ingredients:

- 200g rice noodles
- 1 tablespoon chili oil
- 2 tablespoons soy sauce
- 1 tablespoon rice vinegar
- 1 tablespoon Sichuan peppercorns
- 2 cloves garlic, minced
- 1/4 cup cilantro, chopped
- 1/4 cup chopped peanuts
- 2 tablespoons scallions, chopped

Instructions:

1. Cook noodles and set aside.
2. Heat chili oil in a pan, add garlic and Sichuan peppercorns, then fry for 1 minute.
3. Add soy sauce, rice vinegar, and sugar. Stir to combine.
4. Toss the noodles in the sauce, and top with cilantro, peanuts, and scallions.

Cantonese Beef Chow Fun

Ingredients:

- 200g flat rice noodles (chow fun)
- 1/2 lb beef sirloin, sliced thinly
- 2 tablespoons soy sauce
- 1 tablespoon oyster sauce
- 1 tablespoon Shaoxing wine
- 2 cloves garlic, minced
- 1/2 cup bean sprouts
- 1/4 cup green onions, chopped
- 2 tablespoons vegetable oil

Instructions:

1. Cook rice noodles and set aside.
2. In a pan, heat vegetable oil and stir-fry garlic until fragrant. Add beef and cook until browned.
3. Add soy sauce, oyster sauce, and Shaoxing wine, then toss in the cooked noodles and bean sprouts.
4. Stir-fry for 2-3 minutes, then garnish with green onions before serving.

Scallion Oil Noodles

Ingredients:

- 200g egg noodles
- 1/4 cup vegetable oil
- 1/4 cup sesame oil
- 4-5 scallions, chopped
- 2 tablespoons soy sauce
- 1 tablespoon rice vinegar
- 1 teaspoon sugar

Instructions:

1. Cook noodles and set aside.
2. Heat vegetable oil in a pan and sauté scallions until fragrant.
3. Add sesame oil, soy sauce, rice vinegar, and sugar. Stir to combine.
4. Toss the cooked noodles in the scallion oil sauce, and serve hot.

Stewed Pork Belly Noodles

Ingredients:

- 200g wheat noodles
- 1/2 lb pork belly, sliced
- 2 tablespoons soy sauce
- 1 tablespoon hoisin sauce
- 1 tablespoon rice wine
- 1 tablespoon sugar
- 2 cloves garlic, minced
- 1/4 cup scallions, chopped
- 1/4 cup bok choy (optional)

Instructions:

1. Cook noodles and set aside.
2. In a pot, brown the pork belly with garlic, then add soy sauce, hoisin sauce, rice wine, and sugar.
3. Simmer for 45 minutes until the pork is tender.
4. Serve noodles topped with the stewed pork belly and sauce, and garnish with scallions and bok choy.

Beef Brisket Noodles

Ingredients:

- 200g wheat noodles
- 1/2 lb beef brisket, cut into chunks
- 2 tablespoons soy sauce
- 1 tablespoon rice wine
- 1 tablespoon sugar
- 2 cloves garlic, minced
- 1 star anise
- 1/4 cup green onions, chopped
- 1 tablespoon chili oil (optional)

Instructions:

1. Cook noodles and set aside.
2. In a pot, brown the beef brisket with garlic, then add soy sauce, rice wine, sugar, and star anise. Add water to cover the beef.
3. Simmer for 1-2 hours until the beef is tender.
4. Serve noodles topped with the brisket, broth, and garnish with green onions and chili oil (optional).

Noodles with Shrimp and Scallions

Ingredients:

- 200g egg noodles
- 1/2 lb shrimp, peeled and deveined
- 2 tablespoons soy sauce
- 1 tablespoon sesame oil
- 1 tablespoon garlic, minced
- 2 tablespoons green onions, chopped
- 1 tablespoon chili oil (optional)

Instructions:

1. Cook noodles and set aside.
2. In a pan, heat sesame oil and sauté garlic until fragrant. Add shrimp and cook until pink.
3. Add soy sauce and toss the cooked noodles in the shrimp mixture.
4. Garnish with green onions and chili oil (optional).

Cantonese Noodle Soup

Ingredients:

- 200g egg noodles
- 1/2 lb chicken breast, sliced thinly
- 4 cups chicken broth
- 2 tablespoons soy sauce
- 1 tablespoon rice wine
- 2 cloves garlic, minced
- 1/4 cup mushrooms, sliced
- 1/4 cup bok choy
- 1/4 cup green onions, chopped

Instructions:

1. Cook noodles and set aside.
2. In a pot, bring chicken broth to a boil, add chicken, garlic, soy sauce, rice wine, and mushrooms.
3. Simmer for 10 minutes, then add bok choy.
4. Serve noodles in a bowl, topped with the soup and garnish with green onions.

Spicy Sichuan Noodles

Ingredients:

- 200g wheat noodles
- 2 tablespoons soy sauce
- 1 tablespoon rice vinegar
- 1 tablespoon chili oil
- 1 tablespoon sesame oil
- 2 cloves garlic, minced
- 1 teaspoon Sichuan peppercorns, ground
- 2 tablespoons green onions, chopped

Instructions:

1. Cook noodles and set aside.
2. In a bowl, combine soy sauce, rice vinegar, chili oil, sesame oil, Sichuan peppercorns, and garlic.
3. Toss noodles in the sauce, top with green onions, and serve.

Shrimp Wonton Noodles

Ingredients:

- 200g egg noodles
- 1/2 lb shrimp, peeled and deveined
- 1/2 lb ground pork
- 1 tablespoon soy sauce
- 1 tablespoon sesame oil
- 1 teaspoon cornstarch
- 1 teaspoon ginger, grated
- 2 cloves garlic, minced
- 1/4 cup green onions, chopped
- Wonton wrappers
- 4 cups chicken broth

Instructions:

1. Mix shrimp, ground pork, soy sauce, sesame oil, cornstarch, ginger, and garlic.
2. Place a teaspoon of filling on each wonton wrapper, fold and seal.
3. Cook wontons in boiling water until they float. Set aside.
4. Cook noodles, drain, and place in bowls.
5. Heat chicken broth and pour over the noodles.
6. Add wontons and garnish with green onions.

Taiwanese Beef Noodle Soup

Ingredients:

- 200g wheat noodles
- 1 lb beef shank, cut into chunks
- 4 cups beef broth
- 2 tablespoons soy sauce
- 1 tablespoon rice wine
- 2 cloves garlic, minced
- 1 star anise
- 1/4 cup green onions, chopped
- 1/4 cup bok choy

Instructions:

1. Brown beef with garlic, then add soy sauce, rice wine, and star anise.
2. Add beef broth and simmer for 2 hours until tender.
3. Cook noodles and bok choy, then place in bowls.
4. Pour the beef soup over the noodles and garnish with green onions.

Pork and Chive Dumplings with Noodles

Ingredients:

- 200g egg noodles
- 1/2 lb ground pork
- 1/4 cup chives, chopped
- 1 tablespoon soy sauce
- 1 tablespoon sesame oil
- 1 teaspoon ginger, grated
- Wonton wrappers

Instructions:

1. Mix pork, chives, soy sauce, sesame oil, and ginger.
2. Place filling in wonton wrappers, fold, and seal.
3. Cook dumplings in boiling water until they float. Set aside.
4. Cook noodles and place in bowls.
5. Serve noodles with dumplings and a side of dipping sauce.

Dry Fried Noodles with Vegetables

Ingredients:

- 200g egg noodles
- 1/2 cup carrots, julienned
- 1/2 cup bell peppers, sliced
- 1/4 cup cabbage, shredded
- 2 tablespoons soy sauce
- 1 tablespoon sesame oil
- 1 tablespoon garlic, minced
- 1/4 cup green onions, chopped

Instructions:

1. Cook noodles and set aside.
2. Stir-fry garlic, carrots, bell peppers, and cabbage in sesame oil.
3. Add noodles and soy sauce, toss to combine.
4. Garnish with green onions and serve.

Hong Kong-Style Noodles with Char Siu

Ingredients:

- 200g egg noodles
- 1/2 lb char siu (Chinese BBQ pork), sliced
- 2 tablespoons soy sauce
- 1 tablespoon oyster sauce
- 1 tablespoon sesame oil
- 1/4 cup green onions, chopped

Instructions:

1. Cook noodles and set aside.
2. Heat sesame oil, add char siu, and stir-fry briefly.
3. Add noodles, soy sauce, and oyster sauce. Toss to combine.
4. Garnish with green onions and serve.

Red Oil Noodles

Ingredients:

- 200g wheat noodles
- 2 tablespoons chili oil
- 1 tablespoon soy sauce
- 1 tablespoon sesame oil
- 1 teaspoon Sichuan peppercorns, ground
- 2 cloves garlic, minced
- 1/4 cup green onions, chopped

Instructions:

1. Cook noodles and set aside.
2. Mix chili oil, soy sauce, sesame oil, Sichuan peppercorns, and garlic.
3. Toss noodles in the sauce.
4. Garnish with green onions and serve.

Shanghai Scallion Noodles

Ingredients:

- 200g egg noodles
- 1/4 cup scallions, chopped
- 1/4 cup soy sauce
- 2 tablespoons sesame oil
- 1 tablespoon sugar

Instructions:

1. Cook noodles and set aside.
2. Heat sesame oil, fry scallions until fragrant.
3. Add soy sauce and sugar, stir to combine.
4. Toss noodles in the sauce and serve.

Hot and Sour Noodles

Ingredients:

- 200g rice noodles
- 4 cups chicken broth
- 1 tablespoon soy sauce
- 1 tablespoon rice vinegar
- 1 tablespoon chili oil
- 1/2 cup mushrooms, sliced
- 1/4 cup tofu, diced
- 1/4 cup green onions, chopped

Instructions:

1. Cook noodles and set aside.
2. Heat broth, add soy sauce, vinegar, chili oil, mushrooms, and tofu.
3. Simmer for 10 minutes.
4. Serve noodles in bowls, pour soup over, and garnish with green onions.

Luosifen (Snail Rice Noodles)

Ingredients:

- 200g rice noodles
- 1/2 lb snail meat (optional)
- 4 cups snail broth or chicken broth
- 1 tablespoon pickled bamboo shoots
- 1/2 cup bean curd sticks
- 1/4 cup green onions, chopped
- 2 tablespoons chili oil

Instructions:

1. Cook noodles and set aside.
2. Heat broth, add pickled bamboo shoots and bean curd sticks.
3. Simmer for 15 minutes.
4. Serve noodles topped with broth, snail meat (optional), and garnish with green onions and chili oil.

Taiwanese Beef Noodles with Pickled Mustard Greens

Ingredients:

- 200g wheat noodles
- 1 lb beef shank, cut into chunks
- 4 cups beef broth
- 2 tablespoons soy sauce
- 1 tablespoon rice wine
- 2 cloves garlic, minced
- 1 star anise
- 1/4 cup pickled mustard greens
- 1/4 cup green onions, chopped

Instructions:

1. Brown beef with garlic, add soy sauce, rice wine, and star anise.
2. Add beef broth and simmer for 2 hours until tender.
3. Cook noodles and place in bowls.
4. Pour the beef soup over the noodles, add pickled mustard greens, and garnish with green onions.

Crab Meat Noodles

Ingredients:

- 200g egg noodles
- 1/2 cup crab meat, cooked
- 2 tablespoons soy sauce
- 1 tablespoon sesame oil
- 1 teaspoon garlic, minced
- 1/4 cup green onions, chopped

Instructions:

1. Cook noodles and set aside.
2. Heat sesame oil, sauté garlic, then add crab meat.
3. Add noodles, soy sauce, and toss to combine.
4. Garnish with green onions and serve.

Vegetarian Stir-Fried Noodles

Ingredients:

- 200g egg noodles
- 1/2 cup carrots, julienned
- 1/2 cup bell peppers, sliced
- 1/4 cup cabbage, shredded
- 2 tablespoons soy sauce
- 1 tablespoon sesame oil
- 1 teaspoon garlic, minced
- 1/4 cup green onions, chopped

Instructions:

1. Cook noodles and set aside.
2. Stir-fry garlic, carrots, bell peppers, and cabbage in sesame oil.
3. Add noodles and soy sauce, toss to combine.
4. Garnish with green onions and serve.

Dan Dan Mian (Chongqing Spicy Noodles)

Ingredients:

- 200g wheat noodles
- 1/4 cup ground pork
- 2 tablespoons chili oil
- 1 tablespoon soy sauce
- 1 teaspoon Sichuan peppercorns, ground
- 1 tablespoon sesame paste
- 2 cloves garlic, minced
- 1/4 cup green onions, chopped

Instructions:

1. Cook noodles and set aside.
2. Stir-fry pork, garlic, and Sichuan peppercorns.
3. Mix chili oil, soy sauce, and sesame paste.
4. Toss noodles with sauce and pork.
5. Garnish with green onions and serve.

Stir-Fried Udon Noodles

Ingredients:

- 200g udon noodles
- 1/2 cup chicken, sliced
- 1/2 cup broccoli florets
- 1/2 cup carrots, julienned
- 2 tablespoons soy sauce
- 1 tablespoon oyster sauce
- 1 tablespoon sesame oil
- 1 teaspoon garlic, minced

Instructions:

1. Cook udon noodles and set aside.
2. Stir-fry garlic, chicken, broccoli, and carrots in sesame oil.
3. Add noodles, soy sauce, and oyster sauce, toss to combine.
4. Serve hot.

Wonton Soup with Egg Noodles

Ingredients:

- 200g egg noodles
- Wontons (store-bought or homemade)
- 4 cups chicken broth
- 1 tablespoon soy sauce
- 1 teaspoon sesame oil
- 1/4 cup green onions, chopped

Instructions:

1. Cook noodles and set aside.
2. Boil wontons in chicken broth until they float.
3. Add soy sauce and sesame oil to the broth.
4. Serve noodles with broth and wontons, garnish with green onions.

Shandong Handmade Noodles

Ingredients:

- 200g wheat flour
- 1/4 cup water
- 1/4 cup green onions, chopped
- 1 tablespoon soy sauce
- 1 tablespoon sesame oil

Instructions:

1. Mix flour and water to form a dough, roll out and cut into noodles.
2. Cook noodles and set aside.
3. Toss noodles with sesame oil, soy sauce, and green onions.
4. Serve warm.

Yunnan Cross-Bridge Rice Noodles

Ingredients:

- 200g rice noodles
- 1/2 cup chicken, sliced
- 1/4 cup tofu, diced
- 1/4 cup mushrooms, sliced
- 4 cups chicken broth
- 1 tablespoon soy sauce
- 1/4 cup green onions, chopped

Instructions:

1. Cook rice noodles and set aside.
2. Heat chicken broth, add soy sauce.
3. Place chicken, tofu, and mushrooms in the broth to cook.
4. Serve noodles with broth and garnished with green onions.

Noodles with Sesame Paste

Ingredients:

- 200g wheat noodles
- 2 tablespoons sesame paste
- 1 tablespoon soy sauce
- 1 teaspoon sesame oil
- 1/4 cup green onions, chopped

Instructions:

1. Cook noodles and set aside.
2. Mix sesame paste, soy sauce, and sesame oil.
3. Toss noodles with sauce.
4. Garnish with green onions and serve.

Beijing Cold Noodles

Ingredients:

- 200g wheat noodles
- 2 tablespoons soy sauce
- 1 tablespoon sesame oil
- 1 tablespoon rice vinegar
- 1/2 cucumber, julienned
- 1/4 cup carrots, julienned
- 1/4 cup green onions, chopped

Instructions:

1. Cook noodles, rinse under cold water, and set aside.
2. Mix soy sauce, sesame oil, and rice vinegar.
3. Toss noodles with sauce and vegetables.
4. Garnish with green onions and serve cold.

Stir-Fried Beef Noodles with Garlic

Ingredients:

- 200g egg noodles
- 150g beef, sliced thinly
- 1 tablespoon garlic, minced
- 2 tablespoons soy sauce
- 1 tablespoon oyster sauce
- 1 tablespoon sesame oil
- 1/4 cup green onions, chopped

Instructions:

1. Cook noodles and set aside.
2. Stir-fry garlic and beef in sesame oil until browned.
3. Add soy sauce, oyster sauce, and noodles, toss to combine.
4. Garnish with green onions and serve.

Sesame Oil Noodles

Ingredients:

- 200g wheat noodles
- 2 tablespoons sesame oil
- 1 tablespoon soy sauce
- 1 teaspoon garlic, minced
- 1/4 cup green onions, chopped

Instructions:

1. Cook noodles and set aside.
2. Heat sesame oil and sauté garlic until fragrant.
3. Toss noodles with sesame oil mixture and soy sauce.
4. Garnish with green onions and serve warm.

Braised Pork Noodles

Ingredients:

- 200g egg noodles
- 150g pork belly, sliced
- 2 tablespoons soy sauce
- 1 tablespoon dark soy sauce
- 1 teaspoon sugar
- 1 tablespoon garlic, minced
- 1/4 cup green onions, chopped

Instructions:

1. Cook noodles and set aside.
2. Braise pork with soy sauce, dark soy sauce, sugar, and garlic until tender.
3. Add noodles and toss to combine.
4. Garnish with green onions and serve.

Shrimp Lo Mein

Ingredients:

- 200g egg noodles
- 150g shrimp, peeled and deveined
- 1/2 cup carrots, julienned
- 1/2 cup bell peppers, sliced
- 2 tablespoons soy sauce
- 1 tablespoon oyster sauce
- 1 tablespoon sesame oil
- 1 teaspoon garlic, minced

Instructions:

1. Cook noodles and set aside.
2. Stir-fry garlic, shrimp, carrots, and bell peppers in sesame oil.
3. Add noodles, soy sauce, and oyster sauce, toss to combine.
4. Serve hot.

Steamed Noodles with Oyster Sauce

Ingredients:

- 200g wheat noodles
- 2 tablespoons oyster sauce
- 1 tablespoon soy sauce
- 1 teaspoon sesame oil
- 1/4 cup green onions, chopped

Instructions:

1. Steam noodles and set aside.
2. Mix oyster sauce, soy sauce, and sesame oil.
3. Toss noodles with the sauce mixture.
4. Garnish with green onions and serve.

Vegetable Noodle Soup

Ingredients:

- 200g wheat noodles
- 4 cups vegetable broth
- 1/2 cup carrots, julienned
- 1/2 cup spinach
- 1/4 cup mushrooms, sliced
- 1 tablespoon soy sauce
- 1/4 cup green onions, chopped

Instructions:

1. Cook noodles and set aside.
2. Boil vegetable broth, add carrots, spinach, mushrooms, and soy sauce.
3. Add noodles to the broth.
4. Garnish with green onions and serve hot.

Chinese Egg Drop Noodle Soup

Ingredients:

- 200g egg noodles
- 4 cups chicken broth
- 2 eggs, beaten
- 1 tablespoon soy sauce
- 1 teaspoon sesame oil
- 1/4 cup green onions, chopped

Instructions:

1. Cook noodles and set aside.
2. Boil chicken broth, add soy sauce and sesame oil.
3. Slowly pour in beaten eggs, stirring continuously to create egg ribbons.
4. Add noodles to the broth.
5. Garnish with green onions and serve hot.

Braised Beef Noodles

Ingredients:

- 200g wheat noodles
- 250g beef brisket, cut into chunks
- 2 tablespoons soy sauce
- 1 tablespoon dark soy sauce
- 1 tablespoon sugar
- 2 cloves garlic, minced
- 1 star anise
- 4 cups beef broth
- 1/4 cup green onions, chopped

Instructions:

1. Brown beef in a pot, add garlic, soy sauces, sugar, and star anise.
2. Pour in beef broth, bring to a boil, reduce heat, and simmer until beef is tender.
3. Cook noodles and set aside.
4. Serve beef and broth over noodles, garnish with green onions.

Soy Sauce Stir-Fried Noodles

Ingredients:

- 200g egg noodles
- 1 tablespoon soy sauce
- 1 tablespoon dark soy sauce
- 1 tablespoon sesame oil
- 1/2 cup bean sprouts
- 1/4 cup green onions, chopped

Instructions:

1. Cook noodles and set aside.
2. Heat sesame oil in a pan, add soy sauces and toss in noodles.
3. Stir in bean sprouts and cook for 2 minutes.
4. Garnish with green onions and serve.

Fish-Flavored Egg Noodles

Ingredients:

- 200g egg noodles
- 150g fish fillet, flaked
- 1 tablespoon soy sauce
- 1 tablespoon vinegar
- 1 teaspoon sugar
- 1 tablespoon chili paste
- 1/4 cup green onions, chopped

Instructions:

1. Cook noodles and set aside.
2. Stir-fry fish with soy sauce, vinegar, sugar, and chili paste until cooked.
3. Add noodles and toss to coat with sauce.
4. Garnish with green onions and serve.

Sichuan Sesame Noodles

Ingredients:

- 200g wheat noodles
- 2 tablespoons sesame paste
- 1 tablespoon soy sauce
- 1 tablespoon chili oil
- 1 teaspoon sugar
- 1/4 cup cucumber, julienned
- 1/4 cup green onions, chopped

Instructions:

1. Cook noodles and set aside.
2. Mix sesame paste, soy sauce, chili oil, and sugar.
3. Toss noodles with the sauce mixture.
4. Garnish with cucumber and green onions.

Peking Style Hand-Pulled Noodles

Ingredients:

- 200g hand-pulled noodles
- 150g ground pork
- 2 tablespoons soy sauce
- 1 tablespoon dark soy sauce
- 1 teaspoon sugar
- 1 tablespoon garlic, minced
- 1/4 cup green onions, chopped

Instructions:

1. Cook noodles and set aside.
2. Stir-fry garlic and pork, add soy sauces and sugar, cook until pork is done.
3. Toss noodles with the pork mixture.
4. Garnish with green onions and serve.

Hoisin Noodles with Duck

Ingredients:

- 200g egg noodles
- 150g duck breast, sliced
- 2 tablespoons hoisin sauce
- 1 tablespoon soy sauce
- 1 teaspoon sesame oil
- 1/4 cup green onions, chopped

Instructions:

1. Cook noodles and set aside.
2. Stir-fry duck in sesame oil, add hoisin sauce and soy sauce.
3. Toss in noodles and coat evenly with the sauce.
4. Garnish with green onions and serve.

www.ingramcontent.com/pod-product-compliance
Lightning Source LLC
LaVergne TN
LVHW081459060526
838201LV00056BA/2833